D0534225

Shojo Beat

ANONYMOUS NOISE

Ryoko Fukuyama

Anonymous Noise

Volume 16

CONTENTS

Song 88.....3
Song 89.....34
Song 90.....67
Song 91.....97
Song 92.....127
Song 93.....157

SONG 88
KANADE...
HOW LONG WILL WE GO ON LIKE THIS?
ARE YOU GOING OUT?
WHEN WILL SHE FINALLY UNDERSTAND?
OH.
I IMAGINE ...
OKAY.
YEAH, TO ROCK HORIZON.
WE'RE GOING A DAY EARLY, SO I'LL BE BACK THE DAY AFTER TOMORROW.

TAP TAP
...FINALLY COME TO AN END?
...THAT YOUR FATHER WILL BE BACK BY THEN.
WHEN WILL THIS TIRESOME FARCE ...

SONG 88
ROCK HORIZON, DAY 2
THE SUNSET STAGE, 6:20 P.M.
ANONYMOUS NOISE
SONG 4

"ZERO."
SING FOR HER.
JUST LIKE THAT ONE TIME.
IN FRONT OF ALL THESE PEOPLE WATCHING IN THE POURING RAIN.
SING...
...IN FRONT OF HER.
ZANG

YUZU ...!
THAT'S RIGHT, THIS WAS THE FIRST IN NO HURRY SONG HE WAS ABLE TO SING!
I BET HE'S GONNA GO FOR IT.
HE'S HITTING THIS SONG ...
TWIRL
...EVEN HARDER THAN USUAL!
RAM
WOO

PYOOO!!
OKAY, SERIOUSLY, GUMMI. ENOUGH WITH THE "PYO"...
What is that about?
...ING.
THUD
SHINONOME?!
What happened?
SHE MET MY EYES! SHE'S NEVER DONE THAT BEFORE!
SHE'S DIFFERENT TODAY.
SHE HAS THE AUDIENCE IN HER SIGHTS...
...AND SHE'S COMING AT US, FULL THROTTLE!
WHAT'S THE WEATHER REPORT?
Oof...
LOOKS LIKE WE HIT THE STORM'S PEAK. OF ALL THE LUCK...!
NO. THIS IS PERFECT.

1

Hello, and welcome! I'm Ryoko Fukuyama. Thank you so much for picking up volume 16 of *Anonymous Noise*!

As you can see, I've failed to hand-write the author's columns yet again. And after I'd resolved to do them all by hand this year, no matter what! I'm so sorry.

The columns are due at the publisher in about an hour, and I'm starting to get nervous.

That said, I really hope you enjoy volume 16!

ALL IT EVER BRINGS HER...
...IS FEAR.
DO NOT SING. EVER.
DON'T MAKE ME KEEP SAYING IT, KANADE.
THAT'S A LIE.
I'LL FALL ASLEEP SOON. I DON'T NEED YOUR SINGING.
DON'T.
BUT, MOM, YOU CAN'T SLEEP! I WAS JUST SINGING YOU A LULLABY.
AND IF I WERE TO LOSE YOU TOO...
IF YOU SING, YOU'LL DISAPPEAR LIKE YOUR FATHER DID.

...SHE'LL BE CRYING INSIDE.
AND THE WHOLE TIME...
CONSTANTLY WATCHING OVER ME.
SHE'LL STARE AT ME ALL NIGHT.
...SHE HASN'T SHED A SINGLE TEAR.
SINCE DAD DIED...

YOU HAVE TO UNDERSTAND THAT.
HELLO, YUZURIHA ?
ARE YOU GOING TO BE ABLE TO RETURN TO SCHOOL TODAY?
HOMEROOM TEACHER
LISTEN.
SINGING ISN'T GOING TO KILL ME.
I'M NOT GOING TO DIE IN AN AIRPLANE CRASH...
...THE WAY DAD DID.
COME ON.

IT ONLY GOT WORSE ...
YOU SAID SHE COULDN'T SLEEP UNLESS YOU'RE THERE BESIDE HER...
THAT HASN'T CHANGED ?
AND THE HOME TUTOR WE TALKED ABOUT... THAT'S STILL NOT AN OPTION ?
I'M SORRY.
SHE WON'T LET ANYONE COME OVER.
...HAD BEEN MISIDENTIFIED. THEY WEREN'T EVEN HIS.
NO.
...WHEN WE LEARNED THAT THE REMAINS THEY'D FOUND...
I'LL DO THE YEAR OVER.
I'LL CONVINCE HER TO LET ME.
I'LL COME BACK TO SCHOOL.
LISTEN, KANADE, IT PAINS ME TO SAY THIS, BUT...
I KNOW. TOO MANY ABSENCES.

...TO LEAVE YOKOHAMA CENTRAL.
I WON'T TELL HARUYOSHI AND THE OTHERS...
I DON'T WANT...
...ABOUT WHAT HAPPENED THIS YEAR.
I'LL JUST SAY THAT I STARTED A YEAR LATE.
...I WAS DYING TO PLAY MUSIC WITH THEM.
THE TRUTH IS...
"YUZU!"

I WAS DESPERATE TO GIVE FORM...
...TO THE MUSIC WELLING UP INSIDE ME.
ALL SHE NEEDS TO DO IS ACCEPT THAT DAD IS DEAD.
WHY CAN'T SHE UNDERSTAND THAT?
HOW MUCH LONGER CAN WE GO ON LIKE THIS?
HOW MUCH LONGER?
HOW MUCH LONGER?

OH...
OH NO.
MY FINGERS ...
THEY WON'T MOVE!
BAMI

GRIN
?!
HEY, WHAT ARE YOU—
VSH
VSH
!
BANG

BA
BA
M!
DID YOU SEE THAT?! YUZU RECOVERED IN THE NICK OF TIME!
WHEN YOU'VE GOT TALENT LIKE THIS, I SAY "LET IT RAIN!"
YESSS!
IT IS RAINING.
Has been for a while.
MAN...
THAT'S HOW IT ALWAYS IS.
WHEN I STOP SHORT...
...ONE OF THEM COLLIDES INTO ME.
"YUZU..."

PUTTING THINGS OFF. RUNNING AWAY.

...SAYING I CAN'T. MAKING EXCUSES.

IT'S ALWAYS ME...

YEAH...

...I ASSUMED SHE CAME TO REBUKE ME.
TO TELL ME THAT SHE SAW THROUGH MY LIES.
BUT THEN...
AT LAST YEAR'S ROCK HORIZON ...
AND WHY DID SHE...
...COME HERE AGAIN?
WHY DIDN'T SHE SEND HARUYOSHI AWAY THAT EVENING?
IT'S SO HOT OUT THERE.
COME IN.
BEFORE YOU GRADUATE FROM HIGH SCHOOL...
...I WANT YOU TO SING FOR ME.
WHY DID SHE GIVE ME A CONDITION THAT WOULD LET ME CONTINUE MY MUSIC?

...SHE'S A LOT CLOSER.
THIS TIME...
SHE'S GETTING CLOSER.
EVEN THOUGH I KNOW IT TERRIFIES HER.
AND I'VE JUST...
...BEEN STANDING HERE...
WHY DIDN'T I NOTICE IT SOONER?

...
D...
DAD ?
...WAITING.

YOU FINALLY FIGURED IT OUT?
WELL, KANADE ?

OH...
HERE IT COMES!
THE FINAL HARMONY!
MY THROAT...
OhmiGod!
...IS CLEAR.
I CAN SING.
I KNOW IT.
I CAN SING!

WHAT
...

...THE HELL IS HE DOING ?!
THIS REALLY WILL BE A SHOW TO REMEMBER.
NOT LIKE THIS !!
You're not listen-ing!
IS HE TRYING TO CROWD-SURF?!
CHESHIRE !!!
EEEEEK !
CHESHIRE !!!

AFTER THIS...
...IT'LL BE MY TURN!
WE'LL GET OVER THEM TOGETHER.
AND UNTIL WE DO...
ALL MY MOTHER'S FEAR AND GRIEF...
I NEED TO DO MY PART.

STAFF
ROCK HORIZON

...I'M ENTRUST-ING ...
...ALL OF MY SONG...

...TO
YOU,
ALICE.

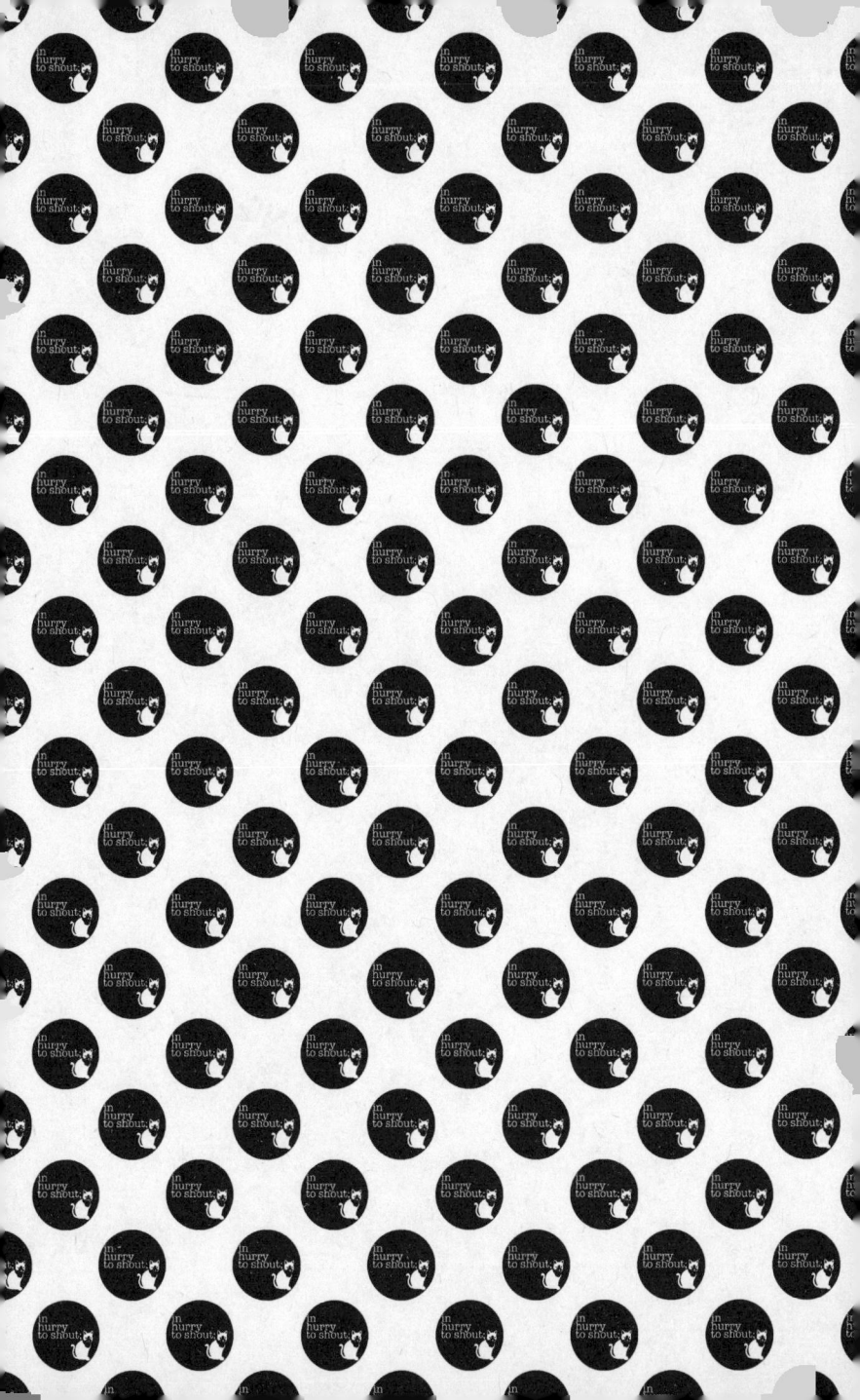
in hurry to shout

SONG 89

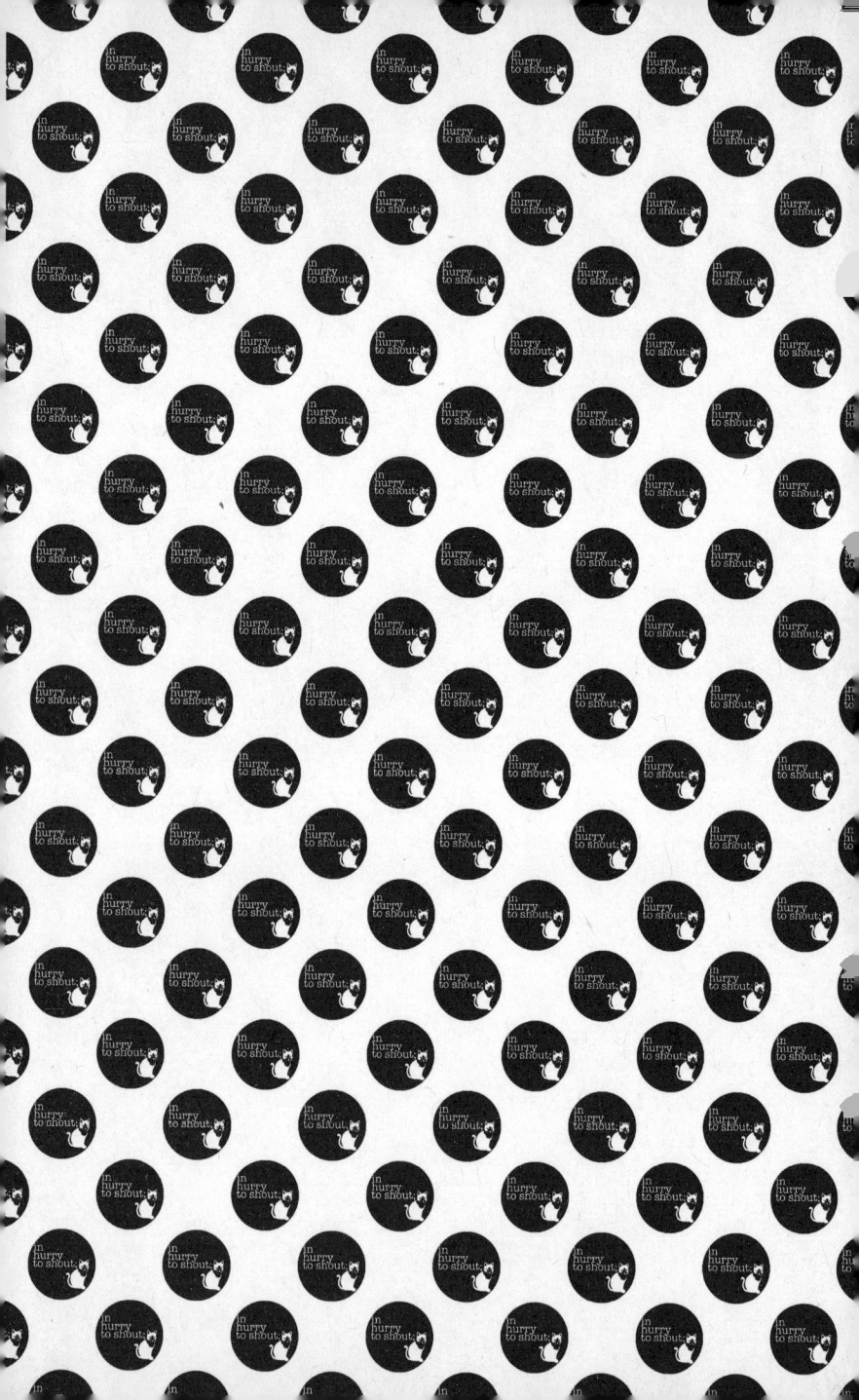
in hurry to shout.

WHO JUST JUMPED OFF THE STAGE ?!
CHESHIRE !
AND SO ...
IS HE STILL IN THE AUDIENCE ?!
I DUNNO! I CAN'T SEE HIM !
BE CAREFUL !
NO RUNNING, PLEASE !
THIS ...
HEY! NO RUNNING, PLEASE !

...IS THE LAST ONE.
STAFF
ROCK HORIZON
WE'RE OUT OF TIME.
WE'VE GOT TO START THE LAST SONG!
HE JUST ...
... SANG ...
ZIP!
YUZU ...

2

Haruyoshi graces the cover of this volume, and those eloquent fingers of his always make him a lot of fun to draw.

Speaking of Haruyoshi, I'm sorry to report that there aren't any Haruyoshi-centric chapters in this volume. To all the Haruyoshi fans out there, I'm so sorry! I'm really eager to draw more Haruyoshi myself… And in fact, Haruyoshi is going to be at the center of the new chapter I'm about to start on for the magazine. So please look forward to that!

THEY PLAYED HIS VERSION TO BUY TIME...
...WHEN I WAS HAVING A MELT-DOWN.
AH, SWEET! THEY'RE PLAYING THE LONG INTRO!
THEY ONLY EVER PLAYED THIS AT LAST YEAR'S ROCK HORIZON!
AND NOW WE'RE PLAYING IT FOR YOU, YUZU.
KRANG

BUT TO GO FORWARD TOGETHER!
...DOTE
NOT TO CALL YOU BACK...
MAINTAINING A CONSTANT STATE...
B-BMP
IT FEELS LIKE THEY'RE ON THE CUSP OF ACHIEVING SOME-THING...
B-BMP
...THAT EVERY ARTIST STRUGGLES WITH.
THEY EXCITE THE CROWD BY BEING RAW AND UN-SCRIPTED.
THEIR STYLE HASN'T CHANGED.
BUT THIS...
B-BMP

SORRY! TIE ME UP!
WHAT ARE YOU DOING?! GET BACK OUT THERE AND PICK IT UP THE SECOND THE INTRO ENDS!
On it.
I COULDN'T HEAR FROM UP HERE, BUT IT LOOKED LIKE YOU WERE SINGING?
...OF TRYING TO CHANGE.
THANKS.
DAMMIT! DON'T GET ME ALL EXCITED LIKE THAT! NOW GO!
I DIDN'T SING. JUST MOVED MY LIPS.
SHOVE
HEY, YANA !
WHAT ?!
THAT WAS YOUR MOM, RIGHT?
IF SHE HEARD YOU, THEN WE'RE SET—
NO.

ROCK
HORIZON
20XX

THE
SUNSET
STAGE

6:25
P.M.

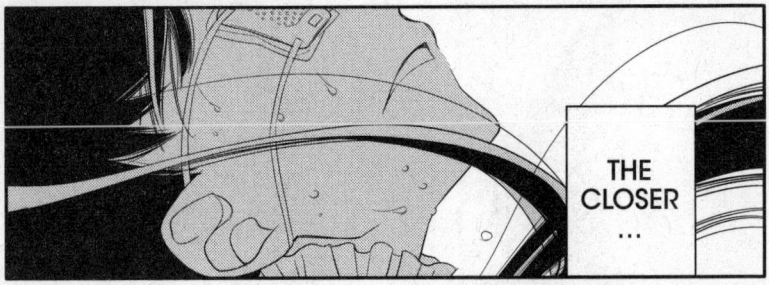
THE
CLOSER
...

BAMA
"HIGH SCHOOL" !!

AH
YOU SOUND INCRED-IBLE!
GASP ...
NINO...
AH
AH
"KANADE..."
"DO YOU LIKE TO SING?"
"THAT POOR GIRL!"
IT'S BEEN YEARS! WHAT THE HELL IS WRONG WITH YOU?
"SHE MUST RUE THE DAY SHE MET YOU!"

AHH, THIS FEELS AMAZING!
JUST INCREDIBLE !!
"I LOVE IT!"
I COULD KEEP ON BEATIN' THESE DRUMS FOREVER!
BAM!
DANG, WHAT A DAY.
SIGH
I WISH IT NEVER HAD TO END.

...AT THEIR FACES.
JUST LOOK...
I'VE BEEN LIVING IN A WORLD THAT BARELY EXTENDS BEYOND MY OWN NOSE.
PLIP
BUT IT'S GETTING BIGGER.
IT'S AMAZING.
I HAD NO IDEA THE WORLD WAS THIS BIG.
I WANT MY VOICE ...
...TO FALL LIKE RAIN.

I
WANT
IT TO
FILL
THE
SKY,
LIKE
SO
MANY
RAINDROPS.

MOMO ...
I THINK I'M READY.
IT'S JUST THE FIRST STEP ON A LONG STAIRCASE.

BUT I THINK I'M READY TO TAKE IT!
LET'S ...
... GOOOOOOOOOO!!!

THANK YOU VERY MUCH!
THE SUNSET STAGE
6:30 P.M.
CHE-SHIRE!
WHOA...!!

WOOO
IN NO HURRY TO SHOUT...
...HAS LEFT THE STAGE.
THEY DIDN'T MANAGE TO FILL UP THE BACK SEATS, HUH?
I DOUBT PEOPLE COULD EVEN HEAR THE LAST FEW SONGS BACK THERE.
Such Bad luck.
AND OF COURSE THE RAIN LET UP THE SECOND THEIR SET WAS OVER.
...
A
A
I ENVY YOU.
BEING ABLE TO DO THAT SUB-CONSCIOUSLY...
OH, ALICE GIRL ...
WE'RE ALWAYS BEST AT PURSUING THE THINGS WE LACK.
ON A SUBCONSCIOUS LEVEL, YOU KNOW THAT.

THAT'S WHY I WANTED YOU TO TEACH ME.
CLICK
THAT WAS SOME STUNT, YUZU. REMIND ME TO CHEW YOU OUT LATER.
GUYS, WOW! BUT NOW I NEED TO HIT THE LITTLE BOYS' ROOM.
I said I'm sorry!
Better get tweet-ing...
ME TOO!

ALICE, YOUR HAIR'S A DISASTER.
ZWAK
YOURS TOO!
AAAH, THAT SET WAS SO FUN!
RIGHT? THAT WAS AMAZ-ING!
FWSH FWSH FWSH FWSH
HEH
LET'S KEEP THIS UP SO WE CAN DO IT AGAIN NEXT...
...YEAR ...

TMP
TMP
...
YOU KNOW ...

I WANT TO KISS YOU...
...ALICE.

YEAH... YOU'RE RIGHT.
SO HERE.
...
DON'T.
NO...
UGH, IT'S HOT!
WHAT ...?
I'M DONE WITH THE BATH-ROOM!
HEY, YOU GUYS GONNA COME WATCH THE FIREWORKS OR WHAT?
HEY !!!
JUST MARKING YOUR NECK.
NYE-H
WHAT ?!
PECK!

THIS WAS IN NO HURRY'S BEST PERFORMANCE YET.
OKAY, BUT FIRST I GOTTA SAY ...
Defo-lutely?
OF COURSE WE ARE!
Y-YEAH, DEFO-LUTELY!
FLUSTERED
YEAH IT WAS !!
ALICE...
H- how dare you!
Nah, you're just old.
My, aren't you full of pep
Hurry up and get changed!
We can still catch the head-liners!

8:05 PM
LINE
AN
I've fallen in love with In No Hurry all over again.
BOOM
EVEN BACK THEN...
...I BET YOU'D ALREADY REALIZED IT.

BOOM
WHEN WE'RE BACK IN KAMAKURA, DO YOU MIND IF I STOP BY YOUR PLACE?
THAT'S FINE.
WHAT FOR ?

HEEEEY, WHATCHU SMILING ABOUT THERE?
NOTHIN'.
HEY, SAKAKI.

BOOM
NEXT YEAR..
...WE'RE GONNA GET THE HORIZON STAGE FOR SURE.

WITH YOUR VOICE AS MY GUIDE ...
WHAT, SERI-OUSLY ?
I'M REALLY SORRY.
COULD YOU NOT STEAL MY LINES, NINO?
BOOM

BOOM

BOOM
...THE MORE IT STRIKES ME...
...HOW PERFECT IT IS FOR YOU.
...I'LL FIND YOU.
DO YOU EVER STOP AND THINK ABOUT WHAT THE WORD "HORIZON" MEANS?
WHERE THE EARTH MEETS THE SKY. OR THE SEA MEETS THE SKY.
Huh.
YOU'RE RIGHT.
THE MORE I THINK ABOUT IT ...
WE'LL MEET AT THAT SKY.
BOOM
BA
WE'LL MEET AT THAT SEA.

I PROMISE YOU, ALICE.

SONG 90

OPENING THEME
"OTHELLO"
IN NO HURRY TO SHOUT
All-You-Can-Me
DIRECTOR: MC
RY EDITOR: KUROIWA
...
OH!

WAA-AAH-HHH-HH!!!
?!

OUR MUSIC ON A TV SHOW... IT'S SO BEAUTIFUL ...
Ngh...
NOVEMBER SOUNDED SO FAR AWAY, BUT IT GOT HERE BEFORE WE KNEW IT!
There, there.
THAT GIRLLESS END-CREDITS TRACK IS GREAT TOO!
THE SINGLE'S OUT PRETTY SOON, RIGHT? YOU TWO MUST BE A BUNDLE OF NERVES!

OUR SONG IS FREAKIN' FANTASTIC.
YUZU IS THE WORLD'S GREATEST SONG-WRITER.

"THANKS."
I so wanna brag to my brother.
Yeah, I bet.
NOVEMBER
WHAT IS WRONG WITH YOU ?!
HUH ?
Don't "huh" me!
AH HA HA
...HAS FINALLY HIT THE AIRWAVES.
IN NO HURRY'S FIRST SOUNDTRACK SONG...
NG THEME
LLO"
HURRY TO SHOUT
IT'S BEEN THREE MONTHS SINCE ROCK HORIZON...
HMM ...
MAYBE IT WAS NOTHING?

IT EVEN HAD A LITTLE BIT OF SEXINESS TO IT, TOO.
DISTINCTIVE AND UPBEAT. PERFECT FOR A THEME SONG.
THEY RECORDED THAT AFTER ROCK HORIZON. NO DOUBT ABOUT IT.

BEEP

EVER SINCE ROCK HORIZON ...
BING
GOOD MORNING, MOMO.
...
MORN-ING.
BONG

Ooh.
THIS NEW IN NO HURRY SONG IS PRETTY GOOD, HUH?
I HATE IT.
NINO'S BEHAVIOR GROWS MORE NORMAL ...
...WITH EACH PASSING DAY.

SO WHAT'S THE VERDICT? YOU DECIDED NOT TO ENTER THAT COMPETITION?
DON'T GIVE ME THAT LOOK.

YOU'VE BEEN IN A SLUMP LATELY, MOMO.
WHAT'S THAT SUPPOSED TO MEAN ?
AHH. TOO SCARED ?

I DON'T NEED THE HASSLE.
IT COULD HAVE BEEN FUN.
THAT'S A SHAME. THAT BAND'S PLAYING AT BUDOKAN NEXT YEAR, YOU KNOW.
NO, OF COURSE NOT. I DON'T DO COMPETI-TIONS.

3

When I was writing the last chapter of this volume, I went to the Tower Records store in Shibuya to gather materials.

The staff were very kind and helpful despite my being a nuisance on two of their busiest days (advance-purchase day and release day), and for that I am deeply grateful. They've been a great supporter of this manga all the way since volume 1, and they're still being amazing even now as we're nearing the end of our run!

(To be continued)

AFTER WE BROKE UP, SHE SEEMED SO PAINFULLY UNCOMFORTABLE AROUND ME.
BUT NOW IT'S AS IF WE WERE NEVER TOGETHER AT ALL.
SAH
"GOOD MORNING!"
I CAN'T SEE THE SKY...

WHAT'S THE DEAL?
I CAN BARELY SEE THROUGH THESE THINGS...
?

IT MAKES ME AFRAID...
...THAT SHE'S ONLY GOING TO GROW MORE DISTANT.

CLINK
WOOSH
CRAP.
MY VISION'S GOTTEN SO WEAK.
I CAN'T SEE ANY-THING...
...AT—
CRUNCH
THIS IS NOT HAPPEN-ING.
MOMO ?
SHA

BLUR
MOMO-VISION
NINO? IS THAT YOU?
YEAH.
That voice ...
WHAT HAP-PENED TO YOUR GLASS-ES?!
Your eyes look all funny.
THEY BROKE.
WHAT ARE YOU DOING HERE?
WHAT—? YUIGAHAMA IS MY NEIGH-BOR-HOOD.
THE QUESTION IS, WHAT ARE YOU DOING HERE?
ME ?
DO I TELL HER? THAT I WAS WRITING A SONG FOR HER?
I WAS JUST LEAVING.
WAIT, MOMO, LOOK—

BONK
...
SORRY ...
I'LL SEE YOU SAFELY HOME.
JUST TO THE STATION IS FINE.
SHA
I'LL GO TO MY OPTICIAN IN KAMAKURA.
THEN I'LL GO THERE WITH YOU.
THANKS ...
YES, IT'S HILARIOUS.
I DON'T MIND. I'M GLAD I RAN INTO YOU.
IT'S KIND OF FUNNY HOW BAD YOUR VISION HAS GOTTEN!
THIS IS HELL.

"Hee hee"?
NOT MUCH FUN FOR ME WHEN I CAN'T EVEN SEE YOUR FACE.
AND BESIDES ...
MONOVISION
I'VE NEVER SEEN YOU LIKE THIS BEFORE. IT'S KIND OF FUN.
Hee hee
I DON'T MIND.
WHAT'S WITH ALL THE COMFORTABLE BANTER?
WHY DOES IT FEEL SO NORMAL?
WE HAVEN'T WALKED SIDE BY SIDE LIKE THIS FOR A LONG TIME.
I WANT ALL OF THIS...
...TO STOP BEING NORMAL. RIGHT NOW.
TAP TAP
TAP
demo1111.mp3
SAVE
TAP!

THE TRAIN TO KAMA-KURA...

...IS NOW DEPARTING.
IT'S PRETTY CROWDED, HUH.
THEY SAID THERE WAS SOME SORT OF DELAY.
MUST HAVE BEEN. IT'S NEVER THIS BAD AT THIS TIME OF—
KA-SHNK
KA-SHNK
OH.

THAT'S THE HAIR PRODUCT THAT NINO ALWAYS USES.
THAT SMELL.
KA-SHNK
...
IT'S, UH... IT'S BEEN A WHILE SINCE WE TALKED, HUH? NOT SINCE ROCK HORIZON.
I GUESS YOU'RE RIGHT. OH, THANKS FOR COMING TO SEE OUR SET.
YOU SPOTTED ME? WE WERE PRETTY FAR BACK.
I SAW YOU. AND MIOU AND THAT DRUMMER GUY TOO.
AH. DRUNKY.
The name's Hojo!
IT WAS THE FIRST TIME...
...I WAS ABLE TO SEE THAT FAR.

KA-SHNK
NO MATTER HOW BIG THE VENUE WE PLAY ...
...I WANT TO BE ABLE TO TAKE IT ALL IN. I WANT TO FEEL EVERY CORNER OF THE PLACE.
I WANT TO BREATHE IT ALL IN AND SING IT BACK OUT.
THAT ROCK HORIZON SET...
BUT NEXT TIME ...
...I WANT TO SEE EVEN FARTHER.
AS FAR AS I POSSIBLY CAN.
KA-SHNK
THAT WAS THE FIRST TIME I FELT THAT WAY.
...WHO USED TO SING FOR ME AND ME ALONE...
THIS NINO BESIDE ME...

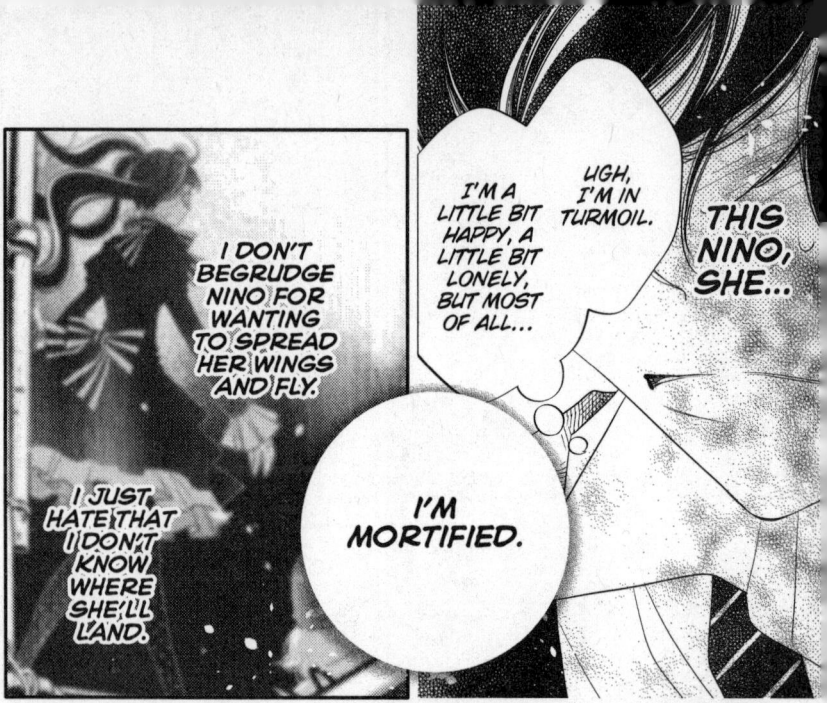

I NEVER CONSIDERED ...

...THAT ONE DAY I'D BE THE ONE...

CHATTER
Oh.
MAY I HELP YOU, SIR?
THESE GLASSES HERE...
I CAN TAKE CARE OF THAT FOR YOU. IT'LL BE JUST A FEW MINUTES.
...WHO HAD FALLEN BEHIND.
GOING WITH THE SAME FRAMES? THIS IS YOUR CHANCE TO MAKE A CHANGE.
I'M USED TO THESE.
THANKS FOR YOUR HELP. I'LL BE ABLE TO SEE AGAIN SOON, SO YOU DON'T NEED TO STAY.
CHATTER
OKAY. BE CAREFUL ON YOUR WAY HOME, THEN.
I will.
YOU TOO.
CHATTER
"AT TIMES LIKE THESE..."

...ONE STEP AHEAD OF—
HOW IS SHE ALWAYS...
THAT WOMAN.
Is that competition still open? If so, I'll
"...WHY NOT SPREAD YOUR WINGS AND TRY SOMETHING NEW?"
Is that competition still open?

SHUP
GAH!

FWP

WELL ...
TODAY IS NOVEMBER 11 ...
...RIGHT ?
I WAS GOING TO SNEAK THEM ONTO YOU AND THEN SLIP AWAY BEFORE YOU SAW ME!
THAT WOULD HAVE BEEN IM-POSSIBLE.
WHAT ARE YOU STILL DOING HERE? I THOUGHT YOU WENT HOME.
DISTRESS
HAPPY BIRTHDAY...
...MOMO.

I REALLY DIDN'T NEED TO KNOW THAT.
IT'S FINE! I WROTE A SONG LAST YEAR. I GET ROYALTIES NOW!
HUH...?
CASHIER
CLERK
Come again!
I THOUGHT I'D BUY YOUR NEW GLASSES AS A PRESENT.
HEY! DON'T PAY FOR THOSE!
...
OH...

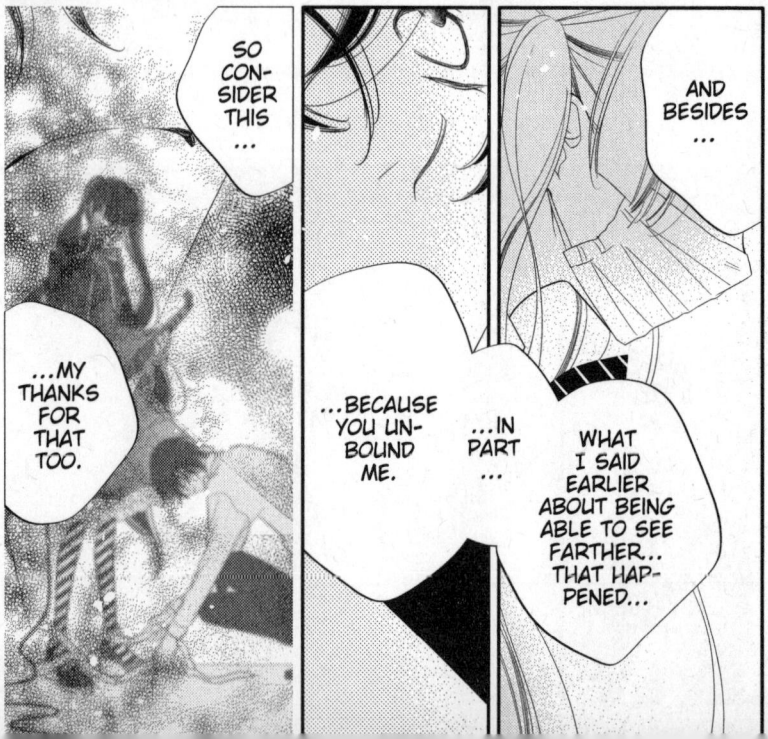
SO CON-SIDER THIS ...
...MY THANKS FOR THAT TOO.
...BECAUSE YOU UN-BOUND ME.
...IN PART ...
WHAT I SAID EARLIER ABOUT BEING ABLE TO SEE FARTHER... THAT HAP-PENED...
AND BESIDES ...

DO IT AGAIN.
WHAT ?
THE GLASSES.
YOU TRIED TO PUT THEM ON ME.
ANYWAY, I'LL GET A CASE FOR THESE.
TUG
PUT THEM ON ME AGAIN.
ONE MORE TIME.

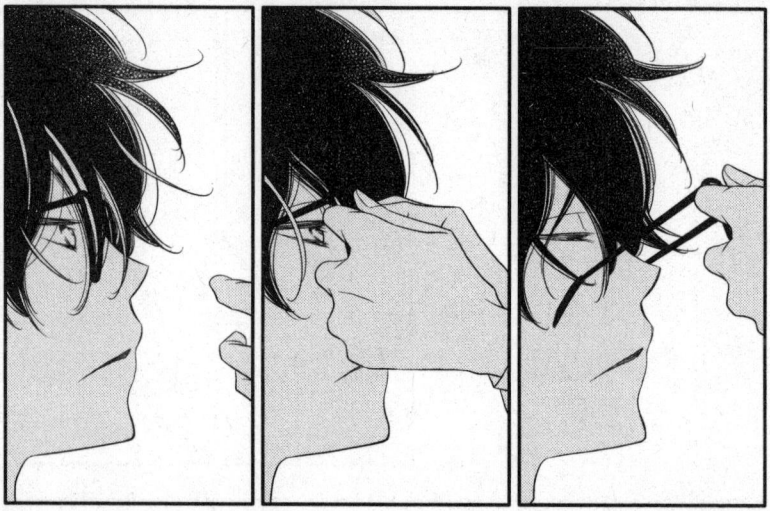

I-SAID I WANTED THIS...
...TO STOP FEELING...
...SO NORMAL.
AND NOW...
SEEING THAT FACE AGAIN...

THE WAY I FEEL IS ANYTHING BUT.
I WANT TO KISS HER...
I WANT TO KISS HER.
...SO BADLY...
PINCH

WSP
THOUGHT I WAS GOING TO KISS YOU, DIDN'T YOU.

THANKS FOR TODAY. TRULY.

I'LL WALK YOU BACK TO THE STATION.
AND, NINO ...
I DID NOT!
WHAT ?!

SO I'M 17 YEARS OLD...
...TODAY, HUH?
I'LL SAVE THAT FOR WHEN WE'RE REALLY BACK TOGETHER.
YOU ARE SO VERY WELCOME.
Grrrr...
Hm hm hmm

EVEN WITH MY GLASSES BACK...
NOTHING.
WHAT ?

...I BET...
HELLO, TSUKIKA ?
IT'S ME.
BUT IF I SPREAD MY WINGS...
...I STILL CAN'T SEE WHAT'S IN FRONT OF ME.
SIGN ME UP FOR THAT COMPETITION.
...I CAN REACH OUT AND GRAB IT.

I'LL GET BACK TO WORK TOMORROW.
I'LL WORK EVEN HARDER...
...FOR IN NO HURRY.
HE TOTALLY SURPRISED ME WITH THAT!
I WAS ALREADY SO ON EDGE...
Hrmph
VRRRRR
"CHERISH IT, NINO."
THE CRISP OF WINTER WAS IN THE AIR...
"HOLD IT CLOSE, AND NEVER LET GO."
IN NO HURRY
Can we meet on the roof after school tomorrow? I've got something to discuss.

...ON THE DAY THAT I SAID THAT.
SORRY I'M LATE.
THIS IS THE ONE DAY I HAVE CLEANUP DUTY!
DON'T WORRY ABOUT IT. WE ALL JUST GOT HERE.
HUFF ...
SO WHAT HAVE YOU GOT FOR US, YUZU?
...
THERE'S SOMETHING I'VE BEEN MEANING TO SPEAK TO YOU GUYS ABOUT...
...EVER SINCE OUR ROCK HORIZON SHOW.
TIME FOR A NEW ALBUM ?
WHAT'S WITH ALL THE FORMAL MEETING TALK?
YANA KEPT BRINGING IT UP THE OTHER DAY.
YEAH, THAT'S RIGHT. SEEMED PRETTY—
I WANT TO PUT ...
...IN NO HURRY ON HIATUS.

...I EVER MADE TO YOU.

SONG 91

"I WANT TO PUT..."

UHHH...
THAT WAS A JOKE...
...RIGHT?

"...IN NO HURRY ON HIATUS."

I'D LIKE THIS SINGLE TO BE OUR LAST.
THAT'S WHAT I WANTED TO TALK ABOUT.
WHAT THE HELL! JUST OUT OF NOWHERE LIKE THIS? ARE YOU TRYING TO GIVE ME A HEART ATTACK?
OH, WOW, HARU-YOSHI. IF YOU COULD SEE YOUR FACE RIGHT NOW...
Heh ?
SPLURK!
ALICE, ARE YOU OKAY ?!
CHAOS
I'VE STOPPED BREATH-ING.
BECAUSE WE'RE DEAD. WE'RE ALL DEAD!!
AH HA HA HA !

...I STILL CAN'T BELIEVE IT.
...I KNEW THIS WAS COMING.
AND YET...
WHAT AM I SUPPOSED TO DO?
B-BMP
How can you laugh about this, Kuro?!
...
ON SOME LEVEL...
B-BMP
MY FINGERS ...
THEY'RE SHAKING.
B-BMP
STOP SHAKING.
So...
DO YOU WANT TO TALK ABOUT THIS?
OR IS YOUR MIND MADE UP, REGARDLESS OF WHAT WE SAY?
No...
I WANTED TO TALK WITH YOU GUYS FIRST.
AND THEN SPEAK WITH YANA AFTER WE'VE HASHED THINGS OUT.
THEN THAT'S A FIRST!

...!
BECAUSE IT SEEMS TO ME THAT ...
...YOU ALWAYS DO WHATEVER THE HELL YOU WANT REGARDLESS OF WHAT ANY OF US THINK.
SO THEN ...
YOU'RE SAYING THAT WE GET A SAY IN THIS, YEAH?
WELL, THERE GOES MY RIGHT TO COMPLAIN ...
I'M... I'M SORRY ABOUT THAT.
CRINGE
MAYBE THERE'S A LESSON FOR ALL OF US HERE!

I THINK I MENTIONED IT DURING THE TOUR, BUT...
THIS IS ABOUT YOUR MOM, ISN'T IT?
YEAH.
I DON'T KNOW IF YOU SAW, BUT SHE CAME TO ROCK HORIZON.
I SAW. SHE CAME LAST YEAR TOO, RIGHT?
MY DAD WAS A SINGER. HE DIED IN AN AIRPLANE CRASH WHILE ON A WORK TRIP.
MY MOM HAS ALWAYS BLAMED MUSIC FOR TAKING HIM AWAY FROM US.
THAT GOES FOR YOU TOO, KANADE.
AND NO MORE WRITING SONGS.
SHE'S BEEN LIVING IN A STATE OF FEAR EVER SINCE.
...MY MOM'S BEEN DRAWING CLOSER TO ME...
OVER THE LAST SIX YEARS ...
DON'T SING...
NEEDLESS TO SAY, SHE WASN'T THRILLED ABOUT ME GETTING INVOLVED WITH MUSIC.

YUZU...
...EVEN IF SHE HASN'T FULLY ACCEPTED MY FATHER'S DEATH.
I WASN'T SEEING THE FULL PICTURE, THOUGH.
SHE STILL HASN'T GIVEN ME HER BLESSING TO CONTINUE MY MUSIC.
HE'S SHAKING.
I JUST... KEPT DOING WHATEVER THE HELL I WANTED, REGARDLESS OF WHAT SHE THOUGHT.
I JUST TOLD HER TO GET OVER IT.
OVER AND OVER AGAIN.

I WANTED HER TO UNDERSTAND WHAT I WAS GOING THROUGH.
BUT I NEVER MADE THE EFFORT TO UNDERSTAND WHERE SHE WAS AT.
YOI NK
BWUH ?!
IT'S OKAY.
GO ON.

HARUYOSHI ...
SO ANYWAY ...
I FIGURE FOR EVERY STEP SHE'S TAKEN MY WAY...
AND I NEED TO TAKE BACK ALL THE TIME I'M SPENDING WITH THE BAND IN ORDER TO DO THAT.
...I OUGHT TO TAKE A STEP TOWARD HER.
IF MY MOM AGREES TO IT, I WANT TO TAKE SOME TIME OFF FROM SCHOOL AND TAKE HER TO AUSTRIA.
MY DAD SPENT A LOT OF TIME THERE, IN VIENNA.
AND FROM THERE, WE'D GO TO ITALY, WHERE THEY FOUND HIS REMAINS.
I WANT TO PUT ASIDE HER CONDITION ABOUT SINGING ...
...AND FOCUS INSTEAD ON GETTING HER TO ACCEPT WHAT'S HAPPENED.

I WANT TO TAKE THE TIME ...
...TO GET HER PAST HER FEAR OF MUSIC.
DON'T GET ME WRONG— I'M NOT QUITTING MUSIC.
BUT I CAN'T HAVE IN NO HURRY AT THE CENTER OF MY LIFE RIGHT NOW.
WHEN I SAY "I'M NOT QUITTING MUSIC" ...
...MAYBE WHAT I MEAN IS "I'M NOT QUITTING IN NO HURRY."
WHEN WE'RE OLD AND GRAY, I WANT TO BE PLAYING GIGS WITH YOU GUYS AT THE OLD FOLKS' HOME!
AT THAT POINT, THE MASK THING MAY NOT COME OFF SO WELL.
AND THEY'D BE HARD TO BREATHE THROUGH.
THEY'RE ALREADY HARD TO BREATHE THROUGH! WHOSE DUMB IDEA WAS THAT?!

4

I have such deep feelings of gratitude about this. To everyone at the Tower Records in Shibuya, thank you!

Working on this manga has taken me to so many places I never imagined I would be able to go. And I don't just mean that physically, but professionally and psychologically as well. And whenever I think about all the opportunities it has given me, you, the reader, are always foremost in my heart. Thank you so much.

...AT NEXT YEAR'S ROCK HORIZON.
WHAT THE HELL WAS THAT FOR ?!
YOU LITTLE—
YOU REALLY—
YOU SON OF A—
WHAK

THAT WOULD BE SUCH AN INCREDIBLE MOMENT!
HOW COULD I POSSIBLY BE AGAINST THAT?!
YOU'RE SHAKING.

STOP SHAKING, NINO.
YEAH, BUT IF WE'RE ON HIATUS, WOULD ROCK HORIZON EVEN INVITE US?
YEAH! DID YOU EVEN THINK THIS THROUGH ?
LOOK!
IT'S A DREAM, ALL RIGHT? SOMETHING TO SHOOT FOR!
THEY SAY DREAMS ...
...ARE MORE LIKELY TO COME TRUE IF YOU SAY THEM OUT LOUD.

I KNOW THIS IS REALLY SUDDEN.
MAYBE YOU SHOULD ALL TAKE SOME TIME TO THINK ABOUT IT.

THAT DREAM ...
IF IT DOESN'T PAN OUT...
...THEN I'M SORRY.

I'VE MADE UP MY MIND.

WILL DO.
I DON'T NEED TO.
GUESS I'LL HAVE TO.
Sigh...
HUH?

WHAT? ALREADY?!
DID YOU THINK ABOUT IT AT ALL?!
WHICH IS WHY...
I DID.

AREN'T YOU GONNA GO HOME, HARU-YOSHI?
AREN'T YOU?

...THERE'S SOMEWHERE I WANT YOU TO GO WITH ME AFTER THIS.
DO YOU MIND?

YEAH. IT WAS THE WAY HE THANKED THE CROWD AT ROCK HORIZON.
IT DIDN'T SOUND LIKE HE WAS PLANNING TO SEE 'EM AGAIN ANYTIME SOON.
CAN YOU EVEN BELIEVE THIS?
EH. I SORTA SAW IT COMIN'.
WHAAAT? SERI-OUSLY?
I GUESS IT HAD TO HAPPEN SOONER OR LATER..
SUCKS THAT IT HAD TO BE WHEN WE'RE RIDING THIS HIGH, THOUGH.
...HAS GOTTA BE YUZU.
SHA...
I GET IT. BELIEVE ME. BUT THE THING IS ...
THE ONE WHO WANTS THIS LEAST OF ALL ...
I WAS THINKING I'D BE PLAYING AT BUDOKAN WHILE I WAS STILL A TEENAGER! NOW I DON'T EVEN KNOW IF I HAVE A BAND!
Siiigh
FUSH

IS THIS WHERE YOU WANTED TO TAKE ME?
I'VE SAID IT BEFORE ...
I FEEL LIKE ALL OF OUR NEW BEGINNINGS START HERE AT YUIGAHAMA BEACH.
SHE
THIS FEELS LIKE ANOTHER ONE.
HUH.
I GUESS SO.
HIATUS APPROVED.
WHAT?! JUST LIKE THAT?!
I UNDERSTAND WHERE YOU'RE COMING FROM, AND I AGREE WITH YOU.
I THINK THIS IS BEST FOR YOUR MOM.
STRAIGHT TO THE POINT
AND I THINK THIS IS BEST FOR YOU.

...I REMEMBERED HOW YOU LOST YOUR VOICE.
DURING THE TOUR ...
AND IT WAS STARTING TO TAKE A TOLL.
...YOU'D BEEN TRYING TO HEAL AN OPEN WOUND THROUGH YOUR MUSIC.
I REALIZED THAT FOR SEVEN YEARS...
I KNOW THINGS ARE BEGINNING TO IMPROVE BETWEEN YOU AND MOMO.
ARE YOU SURE YOU CAN GET BY WITHOUT THE BAND? IT COULD BE A WHILE.
THAT'S WHY I'M GIVING ...
...MY APPROVAL.
A
S
H

I'M SURE.
I SPENT SIX YEARS SEARCHING FOR YOU AND MOMO. WHAT'S ONE YEAR COMPARED TO THAT?
BUT WHO KNOWS WHAT'LL HAPPEN A YEAR FROM NOW?
AFTER ALL, I STILL CAN'T SING—
CAN'T YOU?
SHA

I THINK WE BOTH KNOW...
...YOU ALREADY CAN.

HIS VOICE HAS CHANGED.
THE WAY HE SINGS...
HE ISN'T...
...THE SAME YUZU...
...ANYMORE.
...
HE'S DIFFERENT FROM SEVEN YEARS AGO.
HOW DID YOU KNOW ?

SHA...
THERE'S NO WAY YOU COULD HAVE HEARD ME...
...OVER THE NOISE OF THAT CONCERT.
I DID.
AS CLEAR AS DAY.
BUT WHEN WE CLOSED WITH "HIGH SCHOOL," YOU DIDN'T EVEN TRY TO SING.
AND YOU DIDN'T SAY ANYTHING AFTER-WARD.
SO I FIGURED YOU DIDN'T WANT TO TALK ABOUT IT.
I FIGURED ...
...MY MOM WOULDN'T BE READY TO HANDLE THAT YET.
DON'T START SHAKING.
SO I SANG JUST TO LEAVE MY SONG WITH YOU...
...UNTIL NEXT SUMMER.
DON'T WAVER.

STAY STRONG.
YUZU WOULDN'T DO THIS...
...IF HE DIDN'T THINK HE NEEDED TO.
WHAT'S THIS ?
THAT'S WHY...
A NEW SONG.
I NEVER IMAGINED THIS WOULD BE THE DAY I GAVE IT TO YOU.
I'D LIKE YOU TO WRITE THE LYRICS.
SHA
ARE YOU SURE ?
YEAH.
I WROTE THIS ...
...SO I COULD SING IT WITH YOU, WHEN THE BAND'S BACK TOGETHER.
...I NEED TO DO...

...WHEN HE SHOWED ME THE WAY...
THANK YOU.
I'LL DO MY BEST.
I UNDER-STAND.
...WHAT YUZU DID FOR ME SEVEN YEARS AGO...
WHAT ARE YOU—
WAIT, WHAT THE HELL, ALICE ?!
SHOULD WE HEAD BACK ?
WELL, I GUESS IT'S UP TO KURO AND HARUYOSHI NOW.
...BY PLANTING A BEACON WITH THAT KISS.
YEAH, I KINDA WANNA KISS YOU TOO...
I WANT TO KISS YOU.
SHA

MY MARK ...
...ON YOUR THROAT.
MAY THIS KISS...
...SOMEHOW...

THE ENDING AND THE BEGINNING ...
...WILL BE MY BEACON.
YOUR SONG ...
WE'LL MEET AGAIN, YUZU.
... GUIDE YOU BACK TO ME.
AND FOR THOSE OF US WHO HAVE HIDDEN OUR TRUE FEELINGS...
...ARE ALWAYS TWO SIDES OF THE SAME COIN.

...BEFORE WE MEET AGAIN.

"I'D LIKE YOU TO WRITE THE LYRICS."
"I WROTE THIS..."
SONG 92

SONG 92
"...SO I COULD SING IT WITH YOU, WHEN THE BAND'S BACK TOGETHER."

REALLY? IT'S OUR FIRST DATE IN FOREVER AND THAT'S THE FACE YOU MAKE THE WHOLE TIME?

I'M SORRY I SWEAR ALL I WANTED TO DO TONIGHT WAS FORGET ALL ABOUT MY EXAMS AND EVERYTHING ELSE AND MAKE OUT WITH YOU AND GIVE YOU 100 KISSES AND HOLD YOUR HAND FOR 24 HOURS STRAIGHT AND SHOUT OUT YOUR NAME 200 TIMES!
SOB
PRE-PARING FOR COLLEGE EXAMS
THAT WAS YOUR PLAN? THAT IS STALKER-LEVEL CREEPY!
S!!!-!!!!!-!!!!GH...
WAY TO KILL THE MOOD EVEN MORE.

OKAY, THIS HAS GOT TO BE ABOUT IN NO HURRY. YUZU BREAKING UP THE BAND OR SOMETHING ?
WAAH
WAIT, SERI-OUSLY ?!
NO! IT'S NOT A BREAK-UP! IT'S NOT!
SO IT'S A HIATUS, THEN?!
BULL'S-EYE ★

I BET NINO ALREADY GAVE HIM THE OKAY. THAT GIRL'S DECISIVE, IF NOTHING ELSE.
WHAT, IS THAT A DIS ON ME? YOU'RE SAYING I'M WISHY-WASHY NOW?!
YEAH, BUT I BET EVEN YOU'VE MADE UP YOUR MIND.

YUZU, HE'S JUST ...
HE PROPOSED IT, AND NOW...
HE CAN'T THINK OF ANY OTHER WAY TO DEAL WITH THIS.
WE'RE ALL SUPPOSED TO BE THINKING IT OVER.

YEAH ...
I'VE FIGURED OUT MY ANSWER ALREADY.
I HAVE.

I'LL WAIT FOR AS LONG AS IT TAKES.
AFTER ALL, I DON'T LOVE YUZU BECAUSE OF IN NO HURRY.

I LOVE IN NO HURRY BECAUSE OF YUZU.

RUB RUB
YOU SHOULD TELL YUZU THAT. AND DON'T DILLYDALLY.
DUM DUM DUM DUM DUM DUM
ZWAK
!

AW, CRAP! LUNCH IS ALMOST OVER AND I HAVEN'T EATEN YET!
I'VE BEEN FEELING LIKE I WAS LOSIN' MY EDGE.
HM. IT'S NOT LIKE YOU TO LOSE TRACK OF TIME, EITHER.
YOU'RE NOT USUALLY HERE DURING THE DAY.
Oh.
SORRY, I DIDN'T MEAN TO INTERRUPT.

I GET THAT THIS NEEDS TO HAPPEN ...
...BUT I CAN'T WAIT A WHOLE YEAR.
I DON'T KNOW HOW TO SAY THAT TO YUZU, THOUGH.

AH HA HA. YOU SURE ABOUT THAT?
I'VE FIGURED OUT MY ANSWER.

I haven't been alone with An like this in a while.
AND NOW THAT I REALIZE THAT...
...IT'S MUCH HARDER TO LOOK HER IN THE EYES.
I DON'T WANNA LIE TO HIM. I WANT TO BE SUPPORTIVE ...
DO YOU MIND IF I PRAC-TICE ?
NO! OF COURSE NOT!
NGHH

THE NAPE OF HER NECK...

...SURE IS PRETTY.

ARE THOSE DRUM-STICKS, AN?
YES.
ZOOM
DID YOU SAY SOME-THING?
NOPE, NOTHING! DIDN'T SAY A THING! CERTAINLY NOTHIN' CREEPY!
YOU DIDN'T?
Creepy...?
TURN
THESE DRUMSTICKS WERE USED BY HATTER FROM IN NO HURRY. I WAS IN THE FRONT ROW WHEN HE THREW THEM DURING ROCK HORIZON AND I CAUGHT THEM. RATHER THAN LEAVE THEM AT HOME, I KEEP THEM IN MY CASE SO I CAN BRING THEM EVERYWHERE.
Huh!
Ah, Geez...
WOW, THAT'S REALLY SOME-THING!
I SURE HOPE...
...IN NO HURRY WILL DO ANOTHER SHOW SOON...

WHAT WOULD YOU DO IF IN NO HURRY ANNOUNCED THEY WEREN'T GONNA PERFORM FOR A FEW YEARS?
"...IN NO HURRY ON HIATUS."
HEY, AN...
"I WANT TO PUT..."
I'D WAIT UNTIL THEY DID PER-FORM.
LET'S SAY IT WAS LIKE THREE YEARS... FIVE YEARS, MAYBE.
YOU'D PROBABLY HAVE OTHER FAVORITE BANDS BY THEN.
THAT'S PROBABLY TRUE.
BUT IT WOULDN'T CHANGE THE WAY I FEEL ABOUT IN NO HURRY.

WE LOVED EACH OTHER.
WE DIDN'T KNOW IF WE'D EVER MEET AGAIN.
BUT WE DIDN'T GET SCARED.
CUZ AFTER ALL...
NO MATTER HOW MANY YEARS PASSED.
AFTER THAT DAY...
...WE WAITED YEARS.

HEY, YUZU? YEAH, IT'S ME.
I'M AN IDIOT.

THANK YOU, AN.
HM ?
I'LL BE BACK. I GOTTA MAKE A CALL.
YUP ...

IT'S BEEN A WHILE SINCE I'VE RUN INTO YOU AT THE STUDIO.
THE ANSWER COULDN'T HAVE BEEN MORE CLEAR.
OH, HEY!

MITSU ...
WHY SO SERIOUS TODAY, ALICE GIRL?
I SEE.
NAH, THE BAND'S HERE TOO.
PRAC-TICING SOLO TODAY ?

NO WAY! NOW THAT'S A JUICY NUGGET!
WHAA
OH, MITSU ...
SNIFF...

WHAT HAPPENS TO BANDS THAT TAKE A YEAR OFF?
IT DEPENDS ON HOW WELL-KNOWN THEY ARE, BUT THE DIRECTION IS GENERALLY DOWNHILL.
RIGHT ?!
WHAT, YOU GUYS BREAKING UP OR SOMETHING?

5

Readers of the magazine and my Instagram followers already know this, but *Anonymous Noise* will be drawing to a close over the next year.

The final chapter is expected to run in the magazine just a few months from now. It's really been hitting me hard as I've been writing the final chapters, and that was especially true with chapter 91 in this volume. If you have the time, I'd love for you to reread chapter 1 with that chapter in mind!

ISN'T THAT EXACTLY WHAT YOU'RE BEST AT, ALICE GIRL?

THANK YOU FOR EVERY-THING!
I LOVE YOU SO MUCH!
DASH

MITSU ...
YEAH ?

SPLASH
AWWW! YOU TWO ARE GONNA MAKE SUCH A CUTE COUPLE!
I THOUGHT YOU SAID YOU WERE DONE WITH HER.
AND HERE SHE IS, CONFESSING HER LOVE TO YOU.
SHUT UP.
"CHERISH IT, NINO."
"HOLD IT CLOSE, AND NEVER LET GO."

I'M OKAY WITH IT. THE HIATUS, I MEAN.
ME TOO.

ARE YOU GUYS SURE ?
A WARRIOR NEVER GOES BACK ON HIS WORD!
A warrior ...?
JUST SO YOU KNOW ...

IT'S ONLY CUZ I LOVE YOU.

ZWAK
HOW'S THE MEETING GOING?
SORRY I'M LATE.
YOU TWO ARE CREEPING ME THE HELL OUT RIGHT NOW!
WAY TO HORN IN ON OUR MOMENT, BRO!
OH, KURO! YOU STOLE MY LINE!
SHUDDER
I'M SORRY! NOW, THERE'S SOMETHING I WANT TO DISCUSS.
COME ON, NINO. HOW CAN YOU BE LATE AT A TIME LIKE THIS?
HUFF
HUFF
THEY GAVE ME THE OKAY ON THE HIATUS.
GLENGH
OUR NEW SINGLE?
UM, SO...
NOW YOU'VE CURSED ME!
Not funny!
WE'LL CALL YOU HAIR-NO-SHI!
Hee hee!
FOR THE LOVE OF GOD, WHAT NOW?! I CAN'T TAKE ANY MORE DRAMA! MY HAIR'S FALLING OUT AS IT IS!

I WANT TO TAKE "OTHELLO" TO NUMBER ONE!

ACCORDINGLY ...
I'VE BEEN DOING A LOT OF RESEARCH ON HOW BANDS PROMOTE THEIR SINGLES.
EVERYTHING FROM DEBUT SINGLES TO RELEASES FROM TOP ACTS...
I CAME UP WITH SOME IDEAS FOR THINGS WE CAN DO.
WOW, NINO, THIS IS REALLY ...
ALICE, GEEZ ...
IF WE WANT TO REUNITE AT NEXT YEAR'S ROCK HORIZON...
BAM
WE HAVE THIS SPLIT SINGLE WITH GIRLLESS, RIGHT?
REMEMBER WHAT YANA SAID WHEN I GUESTED FOR THEM AT ROCK HORIZON?
ABOUT HOW THEY HAVE A PRETTY DIFFERENT FAN BASE FROM US?
THIS COULD BE OUR CHANCE TO REACH PEOPLE WHO AREN'T FAMILIAR WITH OUR MUSIC!
AND WE DON'T NEED TO HIDE FROM YUZU'S MOM ANYMORE! SO WE CAN GET MORE EXPOSURE NOW, RIGHT?

...THEN WE NEED TO LAY THE GROUNDWORK NOW WHILE YUZU'S STILL ON BOARD!
...!!
ALSO ...
DID NINOCCHI NOT SLEEP LAST NIGHT?
HER EYES ARE ALL BLOOD-SHOT.
AH, I GET IT.
MORE THAN ANYTHING, WE NEED TO THANK OUR FANS FOR THEIR SUPPORT.
I WANT TO LEAVE THEM WITH AN ACHIEVE-MENT...
SHE'S BEEN RUNNING AT FULL THROTTLE.
I BELIEVE THAT...
...THAT WILL REALLY BLOW THEM AWAY.

...“OTHELLO” HAS WHAT IT TAKES TO BE THE NUMBER ONE SONG IN JAPAN!
SHE'S NOT THE TYPE TO JUST SIT AND WAIT.
I PROPOSE WE TALK TO YANA AND SEE WHAT HE THINKS.
HUFF HUFF HUFF HUFF
EVEN WITHOUT THE COLLABORATION AND PROMOTIONAL TIE-IN IDEAS...
...I'M... CONFIDENT THAT—
KOFF KOFF KOFF
WHOA, ALICE, ARE YOU OKAY?!
PFFT

DOOM
WHAT'S THE DEAL, DISRESPECTING MY MUSIC?!
WHAT ?
ALICE! HEY!
YOU ARE REALLY INTO THIS!
?
AH HA HA HA HA HA HA!
You still alive?
HUH ?
Into what? Negima...?
THERE IT IS! HE'S BAAAACK !
What's that mean ?!
So very Yuzu
What is?!
Why are you crying?
WITH SO MUCH LOVE ...
...RAINING DOWN ON US...
EVERY SONG I WRITE HAS WHAT IT TAKES TO BE NUMBER ONE.

HEY!
...I FIGURED NOTHING COULD STOP US.
I SEE IT WENT WELL FOR YOU.
YOU HEADING HOME, AN?
I AM. WHAT ABOUT YOU?
Perfect timing.
YEP, YEP.
OOH. IT'S REALLY COMIN' DOWN NOW!

I'M GLAD.
YOU LOOKED SO CONCERNED EARLIER.
WELL, I'LL SEE YOU LATER.

SHE'S BEEN SEEIN' RIGHT THROUGH ME SINCE THE DAY WE MET.
S...
See ya...
THAT GIRL'S INTUITION IS SCARY.

YOU DON'T NEED TO BOTHER.
IT'S NO BOTHER. GET ON OVER HERE.
OKAY... THANK YOU.
FWOOMP

HEY, YOU BRING YOUR UM-BRELLA?
I LEFT IT AT HOME.
Whaaat?
HERE, I'LL WALK YOU TO THE STATION.
ONLY A MATTER OF TIME BEFORE SHE'S ABLE TO SEE WHAT'S INSIDE MY HEART TOO.

BUMP

B-
BMP

B-
BMP

I'M
BEGGING
YOU.
B-
BMP

DON'T
SEE
THROUGH
THIS.

MY LOVE
FOR YOU...

...IS GONNA TAKE JUST A LITTLE BIT LONGER.
YOU WON!

AND WHAT EXACTLY DID I WIN?
THE COMPETITION! CONGRATULATIONS.
HUH.
YOU'RE SUPPOSED TO BE HAPPY ABOUT IT.
I'M TOO FOCUSED ON A DIFFERENT COMPETITION RIGHT NOW.
AND BESIDES ...
DING DONG
I HAVE A FRIEND COMING OVER.
OUR LOVE...
KCHAK

...IS GONNA TAKE JUST
A LITTLE BIT LONGER.

SONG 93

MY HUNCHES ARE NEVER WRONG.

かまくら
Kamakura

SONG 93

YOU WANT TO BREAK UP?!

WHAT ARE YOU TALKING ABOUT? YOUR ALBUM JUST CAME OUT!

LOOK, OUR BASSIST HAS COMPLETELY DISAPPEARED.

HE HASN'T COME TO THE STUDIO IN A MONTH. AND HE AIN'T AT HOME, EITHER.

ARE YOU KIDDING ME? THAT'S LIKE THE CLASSIC BREAKUP CLICHE!

IT PRACTICALLY TAKES A MIRACLE TO GET SIGNED AT ALL.

THEY DIDN'T EVEN LAST UNTIL THEIR SECOND SINGLE.

WHOA, YANAI, GET THIS! THESE GUYS SENT IN A VANILLA CHICKEN COVER!

KOFF

ANYTIME YOU WANNA STOP TROLLING ME ABOUT V-CHICK, BOSS, THAT'D BE GREAT.
IF YOU WANT ME TO STOP, LISTEN TO THE DEMOS.
OKAY...
I USED TO PLAY BASS FOR A MASKED BAND CALLED VANILLA CHICKEN.
ALL OF MY COWORKERS FIND THIS ENDLESSLY HILARIOUS.
It gets old.

I LEFT THE BAND RIGHT BEFORE ITS MAJOR-LABEL DEBUT...
...AND THEY KNOW EXACTLY HOW MUCH I RESENT THAT.
Hm...
DEMO TAPES ARE PRETTY MUCH THE LAST THING I WANT TO HEAR RIGHT NOW.

MUSIC DRIPPING WITH HOPES AND DREAMS AND PRIDE.
RUS
TLE
in No hurry to shout:
"Spiral"
https://www.youtube.com/watch?v=XXXX
ts@gmail.com

CLICK
Youyube
Search
in NO hurry to shout: 'Spiral'
Viewed 213 times
TAP
"IN NO HURRY TO" WHAT NOW?
TAP TAP
THEY DON'T LIKE TO YELL...?
WHAT DOES THAT EVEN MEAN?
BAM
BA

B-
BMP
WHERE ARE THEY?
ALL THE HOPES AND DREAMS AND PRIDE...
B-
BMP
WHERE THE HELL ARE THEY?
YANAI? WHAT'S GOING ON OVER THERE ?
B-
BMP
THIS HERE...
THERE'S NO VIDEO.
ONLY DARKNESS. AS IF TO SAY...
B-
BMP
..."WE DON'T EVEN NEED IT."
in NO hurry to shout 'Spira
Viewed 213 times

...IS A STICK OF DYNAMITE.
MY NAME IS KANADE YUZURIHA. I PLAY GUITAR AND WRITE THE SONGS.
Sit down
SO, UH, WHAT EXACTLY IS YOUR CONNECTION TO "IN NO HURRY TO SHOUT"?
WELL, I DON'T SEE HOW YOU'RE GONNA FIGURE THAT OUT FROM A SINGLE SHORT MEETING.
Huh ?
I FIGURED I'D COME FIRST AND MAKE SURE THIS COMPANY IS LEGIT.
Umm...
IN MY EMAIL, I THOUGHT I ASKED FOR THE WHOLE BAND TO COME.
HOO BOY. I FIGURED THEY WERE YOUNG, BUT HE IS LITERALLY A CHILD.

BLUSH!
HM...
MAYBE NOT.
BUT STILL...
HOW OLD ARE YOU?
FIFTEEN. I'M IN EIGHTH GRADE.
HE REALLY IS A KID ...
UNEASY
BY 15, SHOULDN'T YOU AT LEAST BE IN NINTH GRADE?
I WAS OUT OF SCHOOL FOR A WHILE.

"OUT OF SCHOOL"?
AND THE OTHER MEMBERS?
TWO IN EIGHTH GRADE, ONE IN NINTH GRADE.
IF WE WERE TO SIGN YOU, WE'D NEED PERMISSION FROM EVERYONE'S PARENTS. WILL THAT BE A PROBLEM?
MY GRANDMA HAS GUARDIANSHIP OVER ME RIGHT NOW. WOULD THAT BE A PROBLEM?
NOT TO ME.
ALSO, I'D NEED YOU TO MAKE SURE THAT MY MOTHER DOESN'T FIND OUT ABOUT THIS. CAN YOU DO THAT?

6

Well, that about wraps it up for volume 16. *Phew*, it looks like I'm gonna make my deadline in time after all. That's a relief!

What did you think of this volume? I can't wait to hear your impressions! I hope we can meet again in volume 17!

[SPECIAL THANKS]
MOSAGE
TAKAYUKI NAGASHIMA
IKUMI ISHIGAKI
AYAKA TOKUSHIGE
KENJU NORO
MY FAMILY
MY FRIENDS
AND YOU!!

Ryoko Fukuyama
c/o Anonymous Noise Editor
VIZ Media
P.O. Box 11010
San Francisco, CA 94101

HP http://ryoconet/
@ryocoryocoryoco
https://www.instagram.com/ryocofukuyama/

HUH ?
"SPIRAL."
WHAT DID IT SOUND LIKE TO YOU?

THEY'RE KIDS.

...IS TELLING ME THERE'S STEEL IN THOSE EYES.
A PLEA FOR HELP.

I DON'T EVEN KNOW IF THEY'RE MATURE ENOUGH...
BUT MY INTUITION...

MAYBE THESE KIDS...
THAT'S WHAT IT SOUNDED LIKE TO ME.
...AS A SCREAM FOR HELP.
MAYBE NOT SO MUCH A PLEA...
...COULD ACTUALLY SUCCEED WHERE I COULD NOT.
...
MR. YANAI...
WILL YOU...
...STAND BEHIND MY MUSIC?
YEP.

MY HUNCHES ARE NEVER WRONG.
In No Hurry to Shout announces hiatus

"I'LL STAND BEHIND YOU..."

YES, ACTUALLY THE RELEASE IS WHAT I'M CALLING ABOUT.
Yeah.
"I WILL."

HELLO, THIS IS MICHIRU YANAI AT CUBYSTEM.
LISTEN, I WANT TO THANK YOU FOR ALL YOUR SUPPORT.

DUN
Othello / Grayish
in NO hurry to shout/girllless
"...AND YOUR MUSIC."
MAJOR ANNOUNCEMENT!
DUN
DUN
Tomorrow, to celebrate the release of their split single "Othello / Grayish," the four members of In No Hurry and the three members of girllish will be making a series of public appearances throughout the country! Places and times will be revealed throughout the day. Also, stay tuned for a major announcement that evening!
–Y (INHTS Management) #InNoLess
BE KIND, HARUYOSHI. YANA WORKED ALL NIGHT TRYING TO EXPAND OUR PROMOTIONAL PLANS AT MY REQUEST AND NNNGGGHHH... ZZZZ...
WOULD IT KILL YOU TO SNORE A LITTLE MORE QUIETLY, YANA?
GNNGH...
SHE FELL ASLEEP MID-SEN-TENCE!
SNORE

In NO hurry to shout
Hokkaido. Miyagi. Nagoya. Chiba. Shibuya
I HOPE OUR FANS REALIZE THAT ALL THESE APPEARANCES ARE IN CD SHOPS.
OF COURSE THEY DO! THAT'S HOW PROMOTIONAL TOURS WORK, SILLY!
girlless
Okinawa. Fukuoka. Kagawa. Osaka. Shibuya

OH, I DO APPRECIATE THAT. OUR FANS ARE GOING TO EAT THIS UP!
YEAH. THIS WAS GOOD WORK.
TOO BAD THE HIATUS NEWS ALREADY WENT OUT.

KURO, THAT WAY'S EAST.
SORRY, WEST JAPAN! WE'LL CATCH YA AFTER THE HIATUS, I PROMISE!
WE DO THE EAST, GIRLLESS DOES THE WEST, AND WE MEET UP IN SHIBUYA!
Love it!

Zzz...
WHAT, YOU DON'T KNOW EITHER ?
OOH, WHAT COULD IT BE?
So excit-ing!

So...
WHAT'S THIS "MAJOR ANNOUNCE-MENT" TONIGHT, ANYWAY?

OF TEETERING ON UNCERTAIN TERRAIN.
THREE AND A HALF YEARS.
Made it to Okinawa!
THESE FOUR PAINS IN MY BUTT HAVE COME A LONG WAY.
IN THE SPIRIT
He's sure eating this up.
FALLING, TUMBLING AND GETTING UP AGAIN.
TOWER
TAKING BOLD STEP AFTER BOLD STEP.
girlless

Alice!
WE'LL WAIT FOR YOU!
NO MATTER HOW LONG THE HIATUS TAKES!
Squeeee!
They're so close!
That's In No Hurry!
That's really them?!
NO MATTER HOW LONG IT TAKES.

TILL THEY GET BACK TOGETHER...
...I'LL HOLD DOWN THE FORT.
TOWER RECORDS
SNORE

BAM
WOWZA!
IS GIRLLESS ALREADY IN THERE?
NO, THEY'RE JUST ARRIVING TOO.
THIS IS YOUR LAST STOP, GUYS.
GO GREET THE STAFF, SIGN THOSE POSTERS AND TAKE THOSE FAN SELFIES WITH GRATITUDE IN YOUR HEARTS.
IF THINGS START TO GET OUT OF HAND, I'LL TAKE CARE OF IT.
NOW GET OUT THERE AND MEET YOUR FANS!

CHATTER
YANA.
IT'S ALMOST TIME.
AH, SO IT IS.
CHATTER

o shout;
BECOMING ADDICTED TO FAME
Othello / Grayish
HAS ALWAYS LOVED THIS SORT OF THING
Mitsu! Eeee!
HATE THIS
Othello / Grayish

FOR THE TIME BEING ...
...I GUESS THIS IS THE END.
LIKE HELL IT IS.
I'M NOT LETTING THIS BE OVER YET.
HUH ?
AND NOW, OUR FINAL ANNOUNCE-MENT.
IN NO HURRY WILL BE PLAYING OUR FIRST-EVER IN-STORE PERFORMANCE ...
...RIGHT HERE AT THE SHIBUYA TOWER RECORDS NEXT WEEK!

WHAT, THAT'S THE BIG ANNOUNCEMENT? ALICE KNEW ABOUT THIS?!
YOU DIDN'T KNOW IN ADVANCE? EVERYONE ELSE DID.
We're playing the Shinjuku store.
HEH HEH! WE ACTUALLY DID KNOW ABOUT IT ALL ALONG! ☆
FOR WHAT YOU'RE PUTTING US THROUGH, WE FIGURED YOU HAD IT COMING!
HEH ?
YAY
YOU GOT A PROBLEM, TAKE IT UP WITH NINO! THIS WAS HER IDEA!
EXCEPT FOR THE PART ABOUT SURPRISING YOU. THAT WAS HARUYOSHI'S IDEA!
OH, LIKE YOU WEREN'T RIGHT THERE WITH ME !
Ah ha ha!
You totally were!

...
BUNCH OF IDIOTS.
TOWER RECORDS
CASHIER
CASHIER
YEP.
THANK YOU SO MUCH!
STAFF ONLY
JUST A BUNCH OF FOOLISH KIDS.
ALWAYS HAVE BEEN. ALWAYS WILL BE.

I KNOW THIS WAS A LAST-MINUTE REQUEST, AND YOU GUYS REALLY CAME THROUGH—
No, not at all!
WE MOVED A LOT OF PRODUCT TODAY, SO THIS WAS GREAT FOR US TOO.
I'VE ALREADY PLACED A RUSH REORDER.
I PROMISE WE'LL KEEP PUSHING THEM THROUGH-OUT THE HIATUS.
Well then...
YANA.
HEY, GOOD WORK TODAY.
NICE THAT IT WENT OFF WITHOUT A HITCH, HUH?
...
SOME-THING UP?
ALL OF THIS ...
IT'S THANKS TO YOU, YANA.

ALL THESE PEOPLE COMING ALL THIS WAY JUST TO SEE US.
ALL THESE PEOPLE BEMOANING OUR UPCOMING HIATUS...
...YOU'RE ALWAYS THERE BEHIND US, NO MATTER WHAT HAPPENS.
IT'S ALL BECAUSE ...
THAT DAY WAY BACK WHEN...
I'M GLAD IT WAS YOU WHO REPLIED.

HEY, YUZU! COME UPSTAIRS AND CHECK THIS OUT!
'Kay.
ON MY WAY!
There's another display for us!
No way!

YEAH, I'D BE IN TEARS TOO.
What a moment.

WHY ARE YOU HERE ?!
I SAW THE TWEET AND WANTED TO CHECK IT OUT.
I work right by here.
DO YOU NEED A TISSUE ?
NO, I DON'T !
SIGH ...
I GUESS THE HIATUS IS GETTING ME DOWN ...

YOU SAID IT YOURSELF WHEN YOU SIGNED THEM.
"THEY MIGHT MANAGE TO ACCOMPLISH WHAT I NEVER COULD."
BUT SOMEWHERE ALONG THE WAY, YOU STOPPED CARING ABOUT THAT, DIDN'T YOU?
WHY'S THAT ?
YOU KNOW WHY! IT'S A HIATUS! WHO KNOWS IF THEY'LL EVER RECOVER?
THEY'LL BE FINE.
AND THAT'S WHY THOSE KIDS WERE ABLE TO FLY HIGHER STILL.
THAT'S WHY THEIR MUSIC WAS ABLE TO REACH SO MANY PEOPLE.
NOW YOU JUST LOVE THOSE KIDS. THEM AND THEIR MUSIC.
AND THAT'S COMING ACROSS LOUD AND CLEAR.

THEY'LL BE FINE, YANA, BECAUSE THEY HAVE YOU.
urry to s

KUZE ...
YES ?
MARRY ME.
WHAA-AAA-AAAT ?!
UH, SORRY, I DIDN'T MEAN TO—I JUST WANTED TO TELL YOU I LOVE YOU, BUT—
OH! NO! NO NO NO !
DIGGING HIS OWN GRAVE
I DIDN'T MEAN TO SAY THAT NOW EITHER! I'M JUST REALLY SLEEP-DEPRIVED AND—
OKAY.
NO, YOU DON'T NEED TO ANSWER THAT. OF COURSE! I KNOW! YOU DON'T NEED TO SAY ANY-THING—

YANAI ...
DO YOU LOVE ME?
WAIT.
WHAT DID YOU JUST SAY?
OKAY, I WILL.
...
WELL ...
IF I HAD TO SAY ...
I MEAN ...
I DO LOVE YOU.

THEN SMILE.
BECAUSE I'M GOING TO MAKE YOU VERY HAPPY.
ANYWAY, ARE YOU SURE ABOUT THIS? MAYBE YOU SHOULD THINK IT OVER.
I DON'T NEED TO. I'M SURE I'LL MAKE YOU HAPPY.
GASP
WHEEZE
AND BESIDES, I'VE BEEN IN LOVE WITH YOU SINCE FOREVER.
R-really?
NO! I'M GOING TO MAKE YOU HAPPY!
REALLY? CUZ I THINK IT'LL BE ME MAKING YOU HAPPY.
NO! IT'LL BE ME!
Nope. Me.

AND MY HUNCHES ...

...ARE NEVER WRONG.

THAT'S QUITE THE COINCIDENCE.

MY HUNCHES ARE NEVER WRONG TOO.

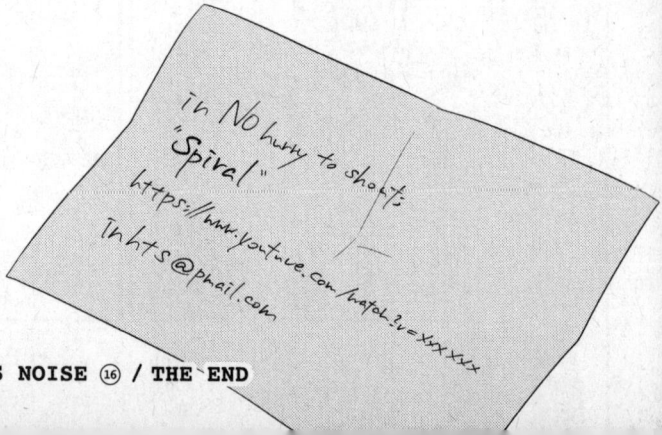

TO BE CONTINUED IN ANONYMOUS NOISE 17

Surprise!

You may be reading the wrong way!

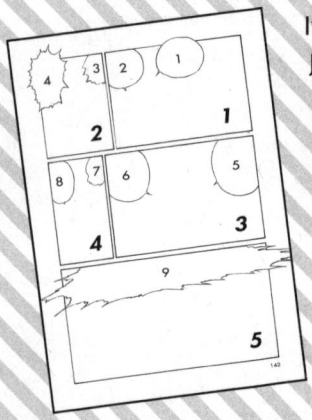

It's true: In keeping with the original Japanese comic format, this book reads from right to left—so action, sound effects and word balloons are completely reversed. This preserves the orientation of the original artwork—plus, it's fun! Check out the diagram shown here to get the hang of things, and then turn to the other side of the book to get started!